THE EVERYTHING KIDS' PRINCESS

PUZZLE and ACTIVITY BOOK

Play, search, and solve happily ever after!

Charles Timmerman, Founder of Funster.com, and Calla Timmerman

Adams Media
Avon, Massachusetts

EDITORIAL
Publishing Director: Gary M. Krebs
Associate Managing Editor: Laura M. Daly
Associate Copy Chief: Brett Palana-Shanahan
Acquisitions Editor: Kate Burgo
Associate Production Editor: Casey Ebert

PRODUCTION
Production Director: Susan Beale
Production Manager: Michelle Roy Kelly
Series Designers: Colleen Cunningham, Erin Ring
Layout and Graphics: Brewster Brownville,
 Colleen Cunningham, Jennifer Oliveira
Cover Layout: Paul Beatrice, Matt LeBlanc, Erick
 DaCosta

Published by
Adams Media, an F+W Publications Company
57 Littlefield Street
Avon, MA 02322
www.adamsmedia.com

ISBN 10: 1-59337-704-5
ISBN 13: 978-1-59337-704-5

Printed in United States of America.

J I H G F E D C B A

This publication is designed to provide accurate and authoritative information with regard to the subject matter covered. It is sold with the understanding that the publisher is not engaged in rendering legal, accounting, or other professional advice. If legal advice or other expert assistance is required, the services of a competent professional person should be sought.
—From a *Declaration of Principles* jointly adopted by a Committee of the American Bar Association and a Committee of Publishers and Associations

Many of the designations used by manufacturers and sellers to distinguish their product are claimed as trademarks. Where those designations appear in this book and Adams Media was aware of a trademark claim, the designations have been printed with initial capital letters.

Cover illustrations by Dana Regan.
Interior illustrations and puzzles by Charles Timmerman.
Chapter opener art by Kurt Dolber.

Contents

Dedication

Dedicated to Princess Suzanne.

Introduction

Mirror, mirror on the wall, who is the fairest one of all? You might think that the answer is Snow White, but this book is packed with princesses and it could be anyone. Turn these pages and you will meet them all: Cinderella, Pocahontas, Sleeping Beauty, mermaids (princesses of the sea), and of course, Snow White. Follow the princesses into a world of enchanted puzzling fun. Along the way you'll journey through castles, play dress-up games, find crowns filled with jewels, kiss a few frogs, and even meet Prince Charming.

The princesses are on a mission: to provide you with nonstop puzzling merriment! They have plenty of clever word games: crosswords, word searches, and more. The princesses also have loads of amusing math and logic puzzles to tickle your brain. They will keep you delighted with entertaining picture puzzles like mazes and hidden differences.

Princesses love to have fun and that is the number one goal of this book! But your parents will be happy to know that your brain will be getting a healthy mental workout. And you can probably find a puzzle or two that will amuse and maybe even stump your mom or dad.

So mirror, mirror on the wall, who is really the fairest one of all? The answer is you, if you try every puzzle in this book! So put on your thinking crown and jump into this magical land of puzzling fun.

Find the Pictures

Can you find each of these pictures on another page of this book?
There is one picture from each chapter.
Write the chapter number in the space below each picture.

___

___

___

___

___

___

___

___

___

Chapter 1

Cinderella

Mixed-up Kitchen

Cinderella's stepmother was very mean and made Cinderella work long hours in the kitchen. Can you help Cinderella find everything in this mixed-up kitchen by unscrambling these letters? The items are all displayed in the pictures on these two pages.

1. etkelt — _Ketle_
2. ekfni — _niffe_
3. onev — _oven_
4. evsto — _stove_
5. onpso — _spoon_
6. rfko — _fork_
7. wobl — _bowl_
8. letap — _Plate_
9. phcrtei — _pitcher_
10. pto — _Pot_
11. pcu — _cup_
12. pna — _Pan_
13. bleta — _table_

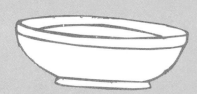

See if you can fit all of the unscrambled words into this clueless crossword puzzle. Each word is used only once, and must fit exactly into the number of boxes.

The Magic Wand

Cinderella's fairy godmother used her magic wand to turn a pumpkin into a carriage. In these puzzles you will change words just by dropping letters.

For example, drop the first letter from this:

and turn it into a nighttime bird with big eyes.
The answer is: **BOWL & OWL**.

Drop the first letter from...

...and turn it into drops from the sky.
t r a i n & r a i n

Drop the last two letters from...

...and turn it into the event where Cinderella and the Prince meet.
B a l l e t & B a l l

Drop the first two letters from...

...and turn it into gorillas.
g r a p e s & a p e s

Drop the first letter from this...

...and turn it into something heartfelt.
g l o v e & l o v e

Drop the first letter from these...

and turn it into something cold
D i c e & i c e

Drop the first letter from a...

...and turn it into a garden tool.

shoe & hoe

Drop the last letter from...

...and turn it into a drink made with leaves.

tear & tea

Drop the last letter from this...

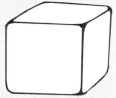

...and turn it into a baby bear.

cube & cub

Drop the first letter from...

...and turn it into what you breathe.

hair & air

Drop the first two letters from a...

...and turn it into a creative work.

heart & ___

Drop the first letter from these...

...and turn them into noisemakers

thorns & horns

Riding to the Ball

Find the path for Cinderella's carriage so that she can get to the ball. The prince is waiting!

Dancing by the Numbers

Dancing at the ball requires some fancy footwork!
What numbers should go in the boxes to complete the equations?

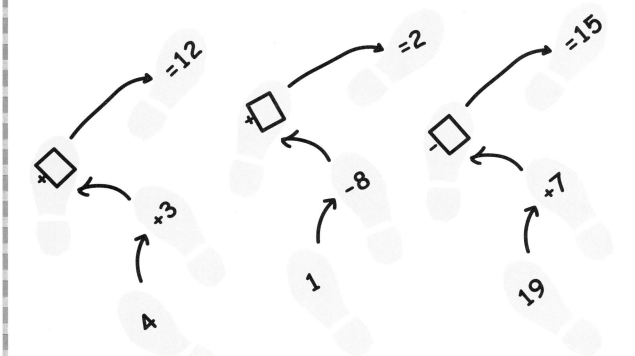

Put a + or - in each box to complete this equation:

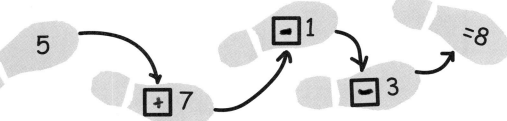

The Last Dance

Cinderella must leave after what song? She wants to dance with the prince as long as possible, and doesn't want to leave in the middle of a song. Her carriage turns into a pumpkin at midnight! Here is a list of all the songs in the order they will be played starting at 10:15pm. Each song length is given as minutes:seconds.

Dream Waltz 15:13

Dance of the Pink Elephant 17:35

Polka Dot Polka 11:58

Foxy Trot 16:47

Orange Tango 18:22

Momma Mambo 14:31

Swing Thing 13:03

Prince Cha Cha Cha 12:49

The Confused Prince

The prince tried the slipper on every young lady in the kingdom. But things are not always as they seem! Can you help the prince figure out these optical illusions?

Which center dot is bigger?

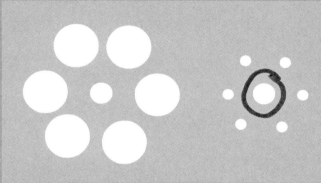

Which horizontal line is longer?

Which horizontal line is longer?

If the Shoe Fits, Wear It!

Draw a line from each footprint to a shoe of the same size. Use a ruler if you need help. Can you figure out which footprint belongs to Cinderella? It is the one that will fit the slipper in the star.

Example of a shoe that fits a footprint:

Wedding Seating

Everybody will be at the wedding to see Cinderella and the Prince get married. You are in charge of deciding who sits where! These four people must sit in the front row:

The Duchess of Duncan

The Earl of Eaton

The Countess of Calypso

The Marquis of Macadamia

Due to royal protocol, the following rules must be followed:
1. An Earl cannot sit next to a Marquis.
2. A Duchess cannot sit next to a Countess.
3. A Marquis cannot sit next to a Duchess.

And of course, The Earl of Eaton must have the Countess of Calypso to his right.

The front row has only four chairs. Write the names of each person below the chair where they shall sit:

_____

_____

the earl of eaton

The _____

Wedding Cake

What shadow exactly matches this silly Cinderella and her goofy prince on their wedding day?

Cryptic Conclusion

Decode this final message. Clue: every letter had been shifted up or down by one. For example, B could be coded as either A or C.

BME UIDZ MJWDC GBQOJMX FWDS BESDQ...

Chapter 2

Pocahontas

My Real Name

The world knows me as Pocahontas, but that was just my nickname. Solve this puzzle to find out my real name. This is the name that was used within my tribe.

1. The first letter in my name is in beam but not bear.
2. The second letter in my name is in eagle and mountain.
3. The third letter in my name is the 20th in the alphabet.
4. The fourth letter in my name is in canoe but not cane.
5. The fifth letter in my name is in animal twice.
6. The sixth letter in my name is in oak but not oar.
7. The seventh letter in my name has already been used twice.

___ ___ ___ ___ ___ ___ ___
 1   2   3   4   5   6   7

Where I'm From

My father was Powhatan, a powerful chief of the Algonquian Indians. To find out what state our lands are in, cross out all of these letters from the grid: ESM

The Time Machine

Pocahontas was born around the year 1595. At that time the printing press and toothpaste had been invented, but not the microscope. Pretend that Pocahontas can fly through time and space. Do you know what she will find?

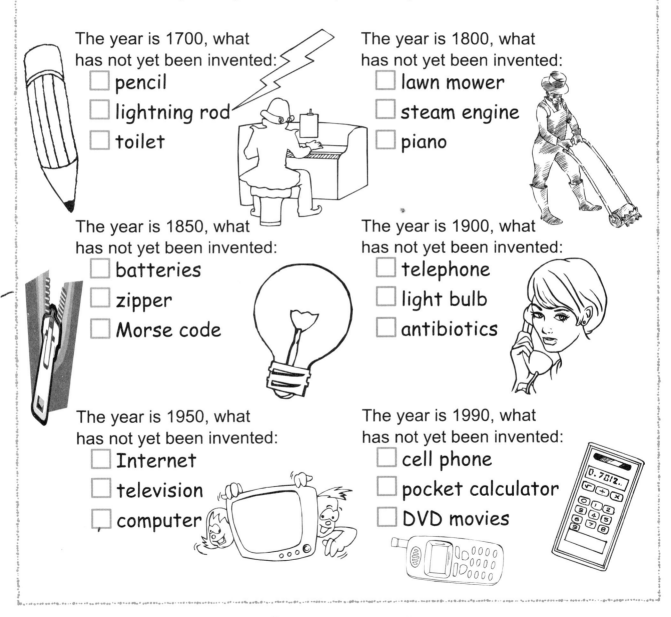

The year is 1700, what has not yet been invented:
- ☐ pencil
- ☐ lightning rod
- ☐ toilet

The year is 1800, what has not yet been invented:
- ☐ lawn mower
- ☐ steam engine
- ☐ piano

The year is 1850, what has not yet been invented:
- ☐ batteries
- ☐ zipper
- ☐ Morse code

The year is 1900, what has not yet been invented:
- ☐ telephone
- ☐ light bulb
- ☐ antibiotics

The year is 1950, what has not yet been invented:
- ☐ Internet
- ☐ television
- ☐ computer

The year is 1990, what has not yet been invented:
- ☐ cell phone
- ☐ pocket calculator
- ☐ DVD movies

The Path to Jamestown

Pocahontas made frequent trips to visit the colonists. Can you find a path from the Indian village to Jamestown where the colonists lived?

Fair Trades

Pocahontas helped improve relations between the colonists and the Indians. Can you help Pocahontas determine which trades between the two groups are fair? Put an equal sign, greater than sign, or less than sign in each box.

These equations show you the value of the goods that were traded.

John Smith and Pocahontas

Legend has it that Pocahontas saved the life of John Smith, a colonist who was captured by the Indians. His life was spared thanks to Pocahontas's impassioned plea.

In this puzzle you will figure out a quote by John Smith. Answer the clues on this page and also fill the letters into the grid on the next page. Work back and forth between the clues and the grid until you figure out the quote. One clue has been solved for you.

A. A large stream of water.

‾‾ ‾‾ ‾‾ ‾‾ ‾‾
17 22 63 27 6

B. A group of players on the same side.

T E A M
4   24 39 13

C. Title at the top of a newspaper.

‾‾ ‾‾ ‾‾ ‾‾ ‾‾ ‾‾ ‾‾ ‾‾
11 60 48 43 28 29 42 31

D. What you get when you boil water.

‾‾ ‾‾ ‾‾ ‾‾ ‾‾
54 21 36 41 23

E. Ten cents.

‾‾ ‾‾ ‾‾ ‾‾
40 51 15 53

F. 12 inches.

‾‾ ‾‾ ‾‾ ‾‾
20 56 16 25

G. Opposite of low.

‾‾ ‾‾ ‾‾ ‾‾
26 62 66 47

H. Bird's home.

‾‾ ‾‾ ‾‾ ‾‾
52 12 55 34

I. Do it at a red light.

‾‾ ‾‾ ‾‾ ‾‾
9   10 32 49

J. To turn over.

‾‾ ‾‾ ‾‾ ‾‾
30 61 64 50

K. Stay out of sight.

‾‾ ‾‾ ‾‾ ‾‾
59 8   37 46

L. Not no.

‾‾ ‾‾ ‾‾
18 38 3

M. Between fourth and sixth.

‾‾ ‾‾ ‾‾ ‾‾ ‾‾
33 2   57 44 45

N. Capable of burning.

‾‾ ‾‾ ‾‾
35 19 58

O. Bees make it.

‾‾ ‾‾ ‾‾ ‾‾ ‾‾
1   5   65 14 7

Pocahontas was a young girl when she rescued John Smith. Solve this crazy formula to determine her age:

$$\frac{\begin{array}{l}\text{number of hours in a day} \\ \text{- number of kings in a deck} \\ \text{+ number of cups in a pint} \\ \text{- number of days in a week} \\ \text{- number of feet in a yard}\end{array}}{= \text{age of Pocahontas when she rescued John Smith}} \, ?$$

1O	2M	3L	4B T	5O	6A	7O		8K	9I		
10I	11C	12H		13B M	14O	15E	16F	17A	18L		
19N	20F		21D	22A	23D	24B E	,	25F	26G	27A	
28C	29C	30J	31C		32I	33M		34H	35N	36D	
37K	38L	39B A	40E		41D	42C	43C		44M	45M	46K
47G	48C	49I	50J	51E	52H	53E	54D	55H		56F	57M
58N	59K	60C		61J	62G	63A	64J	65O	66G		.

Missing Flowers

John Smith has sent Pocahontas flowers!
Which piece will complete the bouquet?

A.

B.

C.

D.

E.

F.

A Vase for Pocahontas

Can you find a vase for Pocahontas?
It must have all of these characteristics:

1. No zigzag stripe
2. One heart
3. One star
4. No flower

21

Mathematical Teepee

Indians often painted designs on their teepees. Can you complete this mathematical teepee? For each empty square, enter the sum of the two numbers beneath it on either corner. One of the examples is already done (3+7=10). Complete all of the squares to the very top.

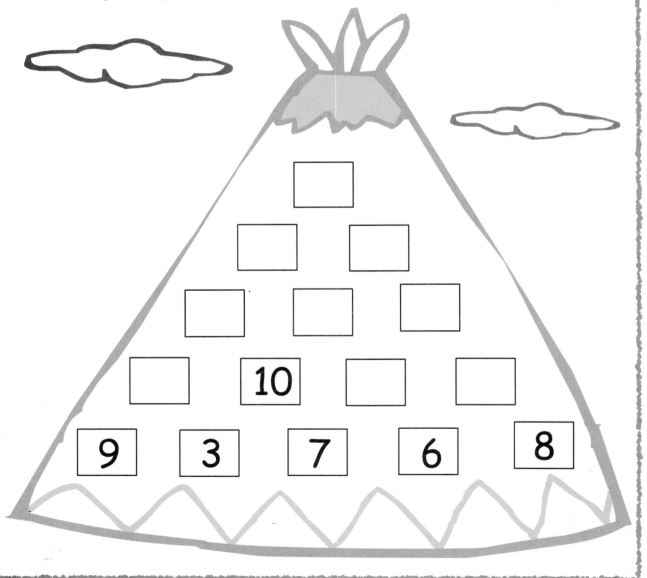

A Corny Pyramid

Can you help Pocahontas turn these corn pyramids
upside down? Move only the given number of ears.
It might help to try to solve this puzzle on a table
using coins for the ears of corn.

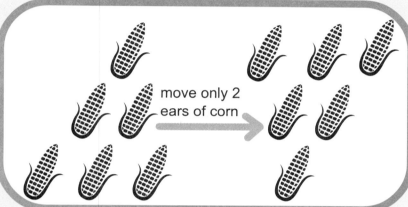

move only 2
ears of corn

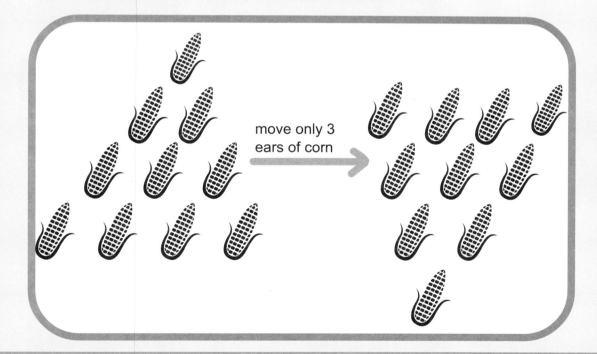

move only 3
ears of corn

Sailing to England

Pocahontas married a colonist named John Rolfe. They sailed to England, where Pocahontas was the center of attention.

Can you chart the fastest course across the Atlantic? Go from start to end along any path. Stop at the circles and add up all of the numbers along the way. The fastest route will be the path with the lowest total.

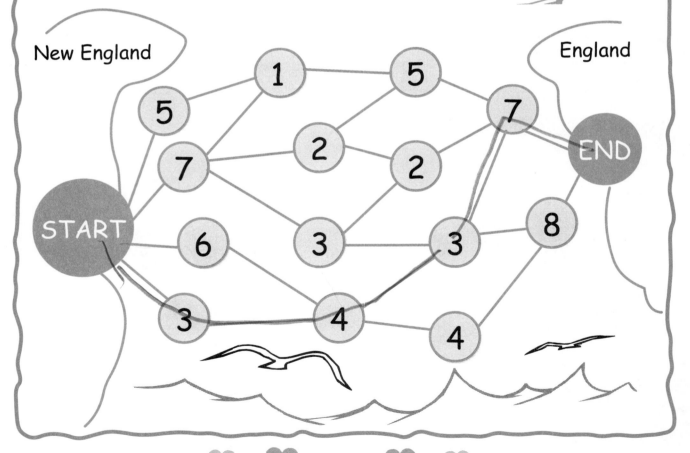

New England

England

START

END

5 1 5 7

7 2 2

6 3 3 8

3 4 4

Mermaids: Princesses of the Sea

Interesting Combinations

A mermaid is a mythical creature with the head of a girl combined with the tail of a fish. Did you know that words can be combined together to come up with new words? For these puzzles determine the common word that can be combined with each of the three given words.

blast_ _ _

_ _ _spring

cut_ _ _

_ _ _ _ball

_ _ _ _print

bare_ _ _ _

bottle _ _ _

hub_ _ _

ice_ _ _

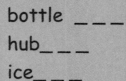

_ _ _ _town

break_ _ _ _

melt_ _ _ _

red _ _ _ _ _ _

_ _ _ _ _word

_ _ _ _ _walk

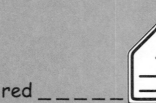

_ _ _burn

_ _ _flower

_ _ _set

26

_ _ _ _stand
side_ _ _ _
_ _ _ _ball

camp_ _ _ _ _ _ _
under_ _ _ _ _ _ _
_ _ _ _ _ _ _ floor

saw_ _ _ _
_ _ _ _pan
_ _ _ _ storm

bus _ _ _ _ _
_ _ _ _watch
door_ _ _ _

_ _ _ _ _house
winter_ _ _ _ _
ever_ _ _ _ _

rail_ _ _ _
_ _ _ _runner
_ _ _ _block

_ _ _ _ _house
_ _ _ _ _weight
flash_ _ _ _ _

outer _ _ _ _ _ _
parking _ _ _ _ _ _
_ _ _ _ _ _shuttle

Mathmagic Mermaid

Some mermaids have magical abilities. This mermaid can work magic with math. Her favorite number is seven. Follow these instructions and she will work magic with your favorite number.

1. Pick a favorite number between 1 and 9.

2. Double the number.

3. Add 7 to the result.

4. Multiply this sum by 5.

5. Now subtract 28.

The lowest digit of your answer is the mermaid's favorite number.
The highest digit of your answer is your favorite number.
How did the mermaid do this?

Transform

It is a common theme in mermaid stories for the mermaid to turn into a human.

Can you change one word into another word in these puzzles? Each step must be a real word and differ from the previous word by only one letter. There are many possible solutions, but try to use only the given number of steps.

Example:
BOY to MAN

B O Y

B A Y

M A Y

M A N

BIRD to BEAR

B I R D

_ _ _ _

_ _ _ _

B E A R

CAT to DOG

C A T

_ _ _

_ _ _

D O G

COW to PIG

C O W

_ _ _

_ _ _

P I G

MOON to MARS

M O O N

_ _ _ _

_ _ _ _

M A R S

HAND to FOOT

H A N D

_ _ _ _

_ _ _ _

_ _ _ _

F O O T

Fishy Friends

Letters are missing from the names of the mermaids' fishy friends. Complete each name by adding one letter. Then find all of the names in the grid of letters on the next page. Look up, down, across, backward, and diagonally. Some letters may appear in more than one name.

Hint: If you're not sure what letter to add, first find the given part of the name in the grid and then you can determine the missing letter.

ShARK	FLOUNDER	PIK_
DAR_ER	YELLOwTAIL	MAR_IN
GUPP_	GOLDFISH	GRUN_ON
BLU_GILL	CAT_ISH	G_OUPER
FLU_E	MINN_W	H_RRING
C_APPIE	ALBAC_RE	BA_S
C_UB	SO_E	PER_H
GOB_	TU_A	STURGE_N
_OD	CA_P	BARRACU_A
	HALI_UT	BULLH_AD
	WALLE_E	TRO_T
	_ADDOCK	MA_KEREL
	ANCH_VY	SN_PPER
	S_LMON	SA_DINE
	GU_TARFISH	M_SKIE
	AN_EL	PA_ROTFISH

E	K	I	P	R	E	D	N	U	O	L	F	Y	H	R
Y	Y	V	O	H	C	N	A	M	U	S	K	I	E	K
E	N	I	D	R	A	S	L	E	I	P	P	A	R	C
L	T	R	O	U	T	N	E	C	H	U	B	H	R	O
L	N	J	A	N	F	A	R	L	S	L	S	S	I	D
A	G	D	L	O	I	P	E	O	I	I	L	T	N	D
W	O	B	B	M	S	P	K	H	F	A	P	U	G	A
D	L	L	A	L	H	E	C	R	T	T	N	R	B	H
A	D	U	C	A	R	R	A	B	O	W	O	G	A	Q
R	F	E	O	S	E	T	M	Y	R	O	I	E	E	C
T	I	G	R	P	I	A	B	P	R	L	N	O	K	L
E	S	I	E	U	R	O	N	P	A	L	U	N	U	E
R	H	L	G	L	G	R	O	U	P	E	R	R	L	C
H	A	L	I	B	U	T	Q	G	T	Y	G	O	F	T
M	I	N	N	O	W	S	H	A	R	K	S	S	A	B

31

Save the Prince

Which rope should the mermaid pull to save the Prince?

Predictions

Mermaids appear in stories from all parts of the world. In many of these stories mermaids can predict the future. Can you predict which bubble will come after the first two?

1.   **OR**

2.     **OR**

3.     **OR**

4.     **OR**

5.    **OR**

Mermaid Riddles

Mermaids love to tell riddles about fish!
Use the pictures to help solve these riddles.

What fish is the most valuable?

Why are fish so smart?
Because they live in...

What fish likes bubble gum?

What fish is the most famous?

Why is it so easy to weigh a fish?
Because they have their own...

Where is My Prince?

This mermaid dreams of becoming human and meeting the prince. She found these scraps of paper in the ocean that have the address of the prince. Help the mermaid by copying each scrap into the corresponding area of the box so that the address will be revealed.

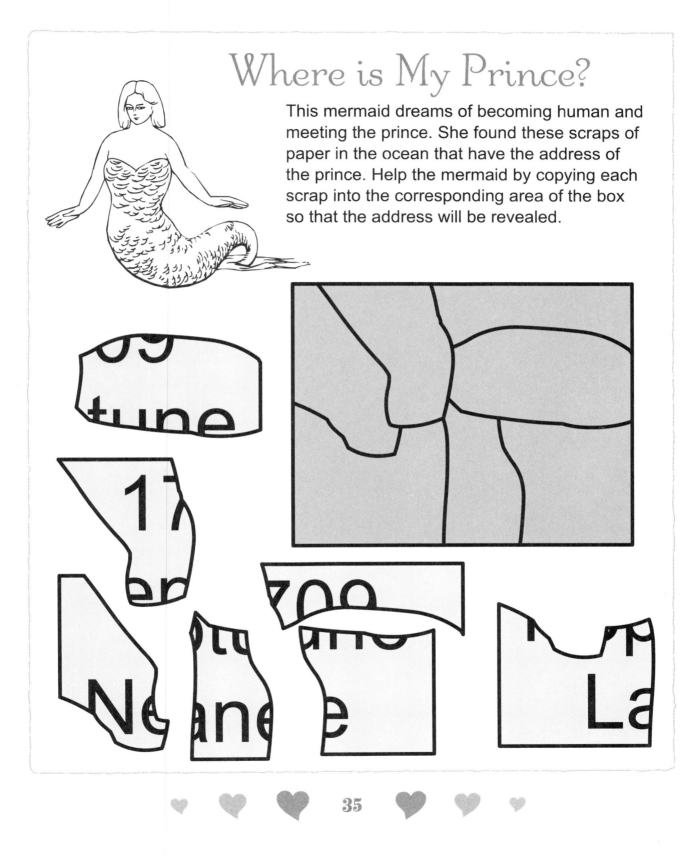

Treasure Watcher

This mermaid keeps an eye on her undersea treasure. Can you find ten things in the top picture that are missing from the bottom picture?

Chapter 4

Sleeping Beauty

Good Fairies

Eight fairies came to see the young princess. Seven were good fairies and brought gifts. One of the fairies was mean and cast an evil spell. Use these clues to figure out which one is the mean fairy:

> Only the good fairies have wings.
> The mean fairy sits on a cloud and
> does not have a star on her wand.

Fairy Gifts

Can you piece together the gifts from the seven good fairies? Each gift is a personal quality that is valued.

What's in a Name?

Using letters in the name SLEEPING BEAUTY, you can make the words LEAP and NAP and many others. Can you find at least twenty words contained in the name SLEEPING BEAUTY?

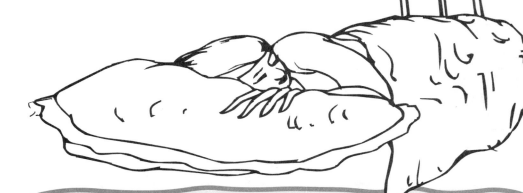

1. _____
2. _____
3. _____
4. _____
5. _____
6. _____
7. _____
8. _____
9. _____
10. _____

11. _____
12. _____
13. _____
14. _____
15. _____
16. _____
17. _____
18. _____
19. _____
20. _____

Spinning Wheel Spell

These spinning wheels have a hidden message for the princess. To read the message, put the letter at the top of each wheel in the first blank. Then move clockwise around and transfer every other letter from the wheel to the blanks until words are formed. The first letters are completed to get you started.

P R I _ _ _ _ _ _   _ _ _ _ _ _ !

_ _ _ _ _ _ _   _ _ _ _ _   _ _ _ _ _ _ _ !

_ _ _

Dreaming Beauty

There are 50 hearts hidden on this page.
Can you circle all of them?

One Hundred Years

Sleeping Beauty slept for one hundred years. Find all of the columns and rows in this castle wall where the numbers add up to exactly one hundred. One of the answers has already been found.

25	18	16	10	21	7	18
7	20	23	10	9	24	4
8	27	7	0	15	12	12
25	3	4	22	24	5	17
16	5	12	18	11	9	22
7	4	27	10	9	20	23
12	10	15	0	11	24	5

Double E

Just like Sleeping Beauty, everything on these two pages has a double E. Can you fill in all of the blanks with letters so that each item is named?

_ E E _ _ _ _

n e e D L e

_ E E

_ _ E E

_ _ E E _

W _ E E _

_ E E _

_ E E _ _

_ _ E E _

_ _ E E _ _

_ E E _ _

_ E E _ _ _ _

_ E E _ _

The Path to Sleeping Beauty

Can you help the prince find the correct path to sleeping beauty's castle? The prince should follow the path that has all 14 letters in SLEEPING BEAUTY.

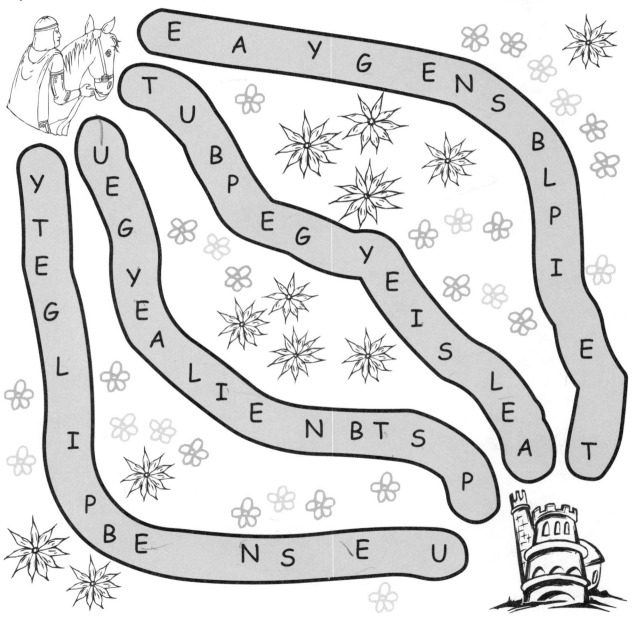

The prince has found the castle! Can you help him find a path through the castle to Sleeping Beauty?

Castle Maze

START

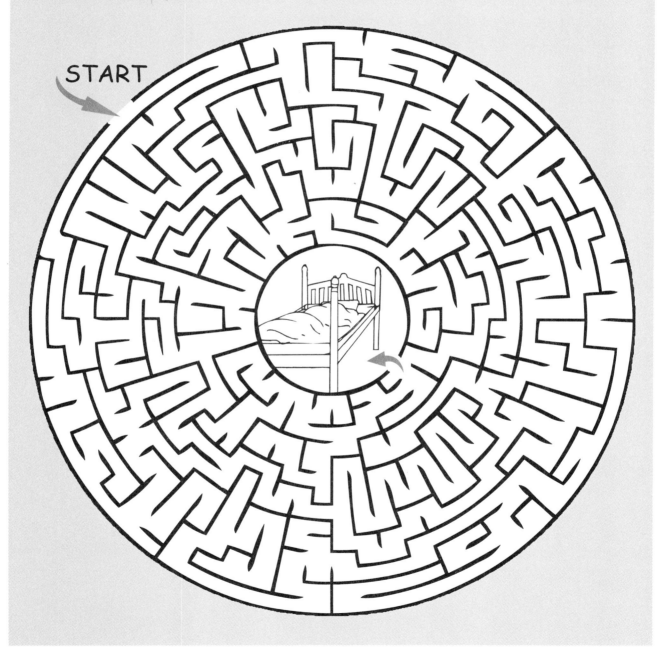

A Message from the Prince

Sleeping Beauty awoke after the prince kissed her. The prince immediately sent a secret message back to the king and queen. Help them figure out the message by putting the letters into the grid. Each letter has a symbol and a number to tell you where it should go in the grid. One letter has already been entered.

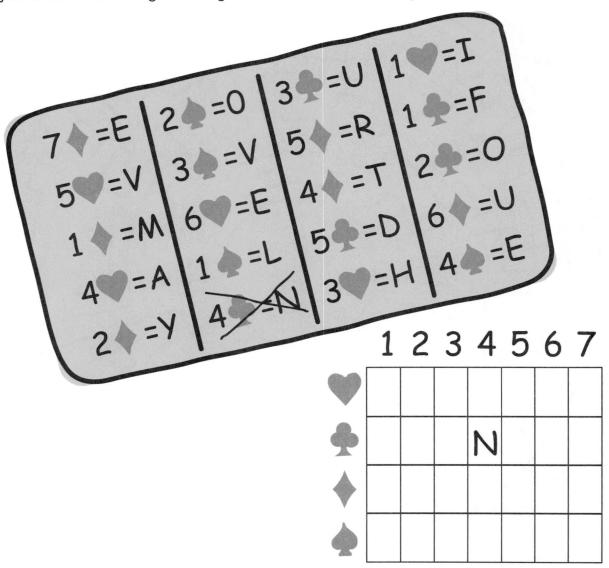

Chapter 5

Snow White

Mirror, Mirror

The queen was furious when her talking mirror said that Snow White was the fairest in the land! Can you find ten differences between these mirror images of Snow White working in the kitchen?

Snow White has two apples, a lemon, and a banana. She put them in a row so that neither apple is on an end and the banana is directly to the right of an apple. List the fruit from left to right.

Snow White has three forks and two knives. She put them in a row so that no fork was next to another fork. List the order of forks and knives from left to right.

The Secret Answer

The Queen asked, "Mirror, mirror, on the wall, who is the fairest one of all?" Knowing the answer would anger the queen, the mirror displayed the answer in code. Can you figure out the answer? A substitution code is used where 1=A, 2=B, and so on.

```
___ ___ ___ ___      ___ ___ ___ ___ ___
19  14  15  23       23   8   9  20   5

       ___ ___        ___
        9  19          1

   ___ ___ ___ ___ ___ ___ ___ ___
   20   8  15  21  19   1  14   4

   ___ ___ ___ ___ ___     ___ ___ ___ ___ ___ ___
   20   9  13   5  19       6   1   9  18   5  18

   ___ ___ ___ ___      ___ ___ ___!
   20   8   1  14       25  15  21
```

Twisty Walk

Snow White fled through the forest to escape the evil queen.
Can you find the path to the dwarfs' cottage?

START

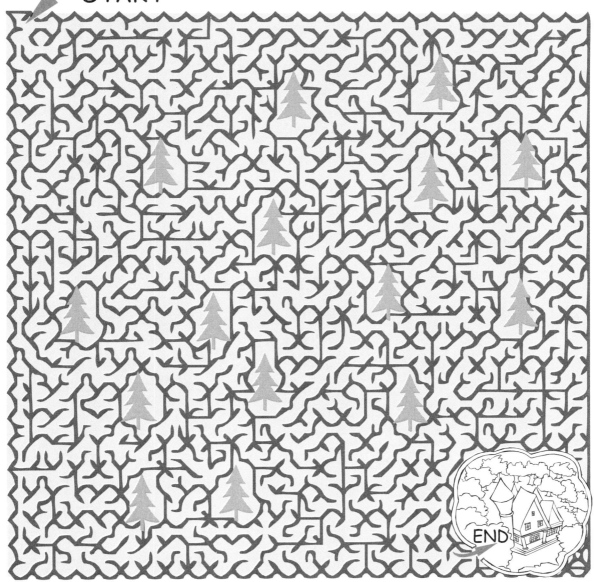

END

Things in the Forest

Can you find the things Snow White saw in the forest?
Look up, down, across, backward, and diagonally.

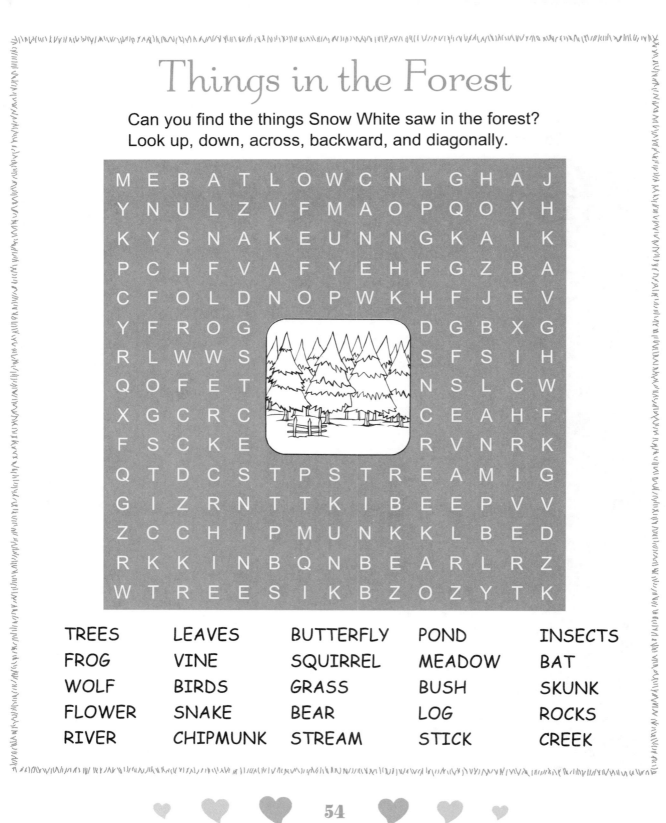

M	E	B	A	T	L	O	W	C	N	L	G	H	A	J
Y	N	U	L	Z	V	F	M	A	O	P	Q	O	Y	H
K	Y	S	N	A	K	E	U	N	N	G	K	A	I	K
P	C	H	F	V	A	F	Y	E	H	F	G	Z	B	A
C	F	O	L	D	N	O	P	W	K	H	F	J	E	V
Y	F	R	O	G						D	G	B	X	G
R	L	W	W	S						S	F	S	I	H
Q	O	F	E	T						N	S	L	C	W
X	G	C	R	C						C	E	A	H	F
F	S	C	K	E						R	V	N	R	K
Q	T	D	C	S	T	P	S	T	R	E	A	M	I	G
G	I	Z	R	N	T	T	K	I	B	E	E	P	V	V
Z	C	C	H	I	P	M	U	N	K	K	L	B	E	D
R	K	K	I	N	B	Q	N	B	E	A	R	L	R	Z
W	T	R	E	E	S	I	K	B	Z	O	Z	Y	T	K

TREES   LEAVES   BUTTERFLY   POND   INSECTS

FROG   VINE   SQUIRREL   MEADOW   BAT

WOLF   BIRDS   GRASS   BUSH   SKUNK

FLOWER   SNAKE   BEAR   LOG   ROCKS

RIVER   CHIPMUNK   STREAM   STICK   CREEK

Seven of Everything

There are seven of everything in the dwarf's cottage. Find the three items on this page that do not have exactly seven copies.

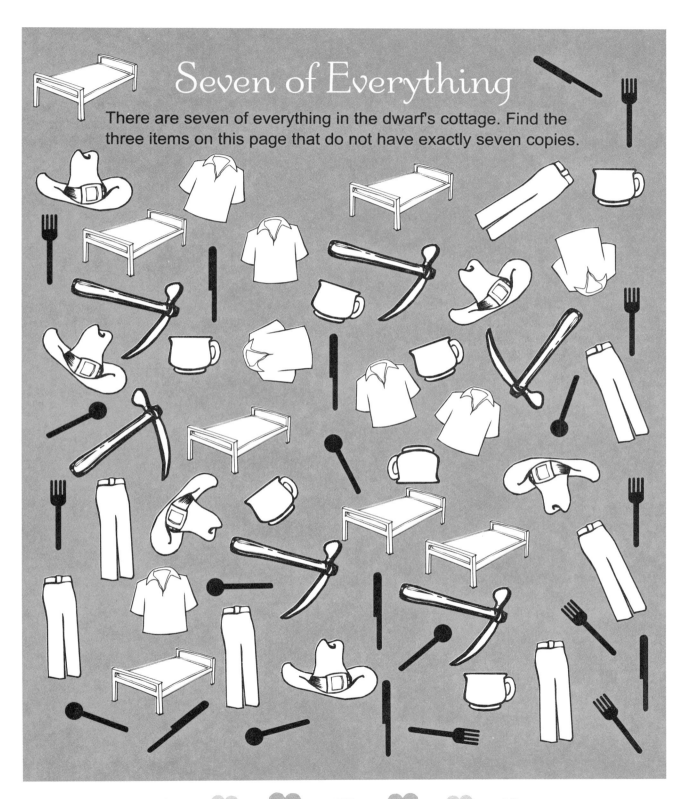

Snow White's Crossword

The dwarfs adored Snow White. They made this crossword puzzle for her with words that use only letters from her name: SNOW WHITE.

ACROSS

2 It's printed in the paper
4 What you do on a chair
6 Smart like an owl
9 Informal letter, maybe passed in class
10 The color of milk
12 Red temperature
14 Gardening tool with a flat blade
15 If loud it can wake you
16 Rock
17 Catches fish
19 Falls in flakes
21 Here is a _____: it starts with the letter H
23 Covered with water
25 Used for smelling
27 Hearty soup
29 548 minus 547
30 Father's boy

DOWN

1 One of two identical babies
3 Annoying cry
4 Worn on the feet
5 210 divided by 21
7 Seen in a theater
8 Short version of hello
11 Truthful, like Abe
12 Carries water to a sprinkler
13 The first even number after one
14 Female chicken
18 Like a city only smaller
20 Direction away from east
21 To strike
22 Bird's home
24 Pulling a car with a truck
26 Very heavy unit of weight
27 To use a needle and thread
28 Make a _____ at the well.

Doesn't Belong

Can you pick out the one equation for each dwarf that doesn't belong?

A. 5 + 2 =
B. 11 - 4 =
C. 3 × 2 =
D. 35 ÷ 5 =

A. 3 × 3 × 8 =
B. 99 ÷ 3 =
C. 59 + 5 + 6 + 2 =
D. 98 - 26 =

A. 37 + 6 =
B. 22 × 2 =
C. 62 - 19 =
D. 86 ÷ 2 =

A. 25 × 2 =
B. 2 + 1 + 2 =
C. 55 ÷ 11 =
D. 100 - 95 =

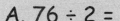

A. 5 × 5 =
B. 15 + 10 =
C. 100 - 75 =
D. 30 -3 =

A. 93 + 3 + 4 =
B. 500 ÷ 5 =
C. 10 × 10 =
D. 102 - 3 =

A. 76 ÷ 2 =
B. 21 + 27 =
C. 19 × 2 =
D. 50 - 12 =

The Poisoned Apple

The evil queen has turned herself into an old woman selling apples. She has a poisoned apple for Snow White. Follow the clues to figure out which apple is poisoned.

1. The poisoned apple is in a row with a turtle.
2. The poisoned apple does not have a heart below it.
3. The poisoned apple is not in the middle column.

Wedding Cake

The prince rescued Snow White and they were married! At the wedding celebration they had a three-layer cake and three tables. Each table had one cake layer to divide however they saw fit. Can you figure out who sat at what table based on the size of their piece of cake?

Table A has 5 seats:

1 _____
2 _____
3 _____
4 _____
5 _____

Table B has 3 seats:

1 _____
2 _____
3 _____

Table C has 4 seats:

1 _____
2 _____
3 _____
4 _____

Diane had 1/8 of a layer.
Emma had 1/3 of a layer.
Shawn had 1/3 of a layer.
Mary had 3/10 of a layer.
Donnie had 1/4 of a layer.
Dave had 2/5 of a layer.
Nick had 1/6 of a layer.
Laura had 1/6 of a layer.
Therese had 1/8 of a layer.
Steve had 1/4 of a layer.
Violet had 3/10 of a layer.
Suzanne had 1/4 of a layer.

Chapter 6

Prince Charmings

Prince Names from A to Z

Add one letter to complete these names. Each letter from A to Z is used only once, so cross them off once you use them:

A B C D E F G H I J K L M
N O P Q R S T U V W X Y Z

Ivan
Samuel
Logan
Paul
Quincy
Hunter
Kenneth
Carlos
Dylan
Oscar
Garrett
Nannick
Zachary

Timothy
Marcus
Noah
Ulysses
Yan
Franklin
Raymond
Jason
Andrew
William
Xavier
Victor
Benjamin

Clueless Princes

Once you figure out all 26 of the names, try and fit them into this clueless crossword puzzle. Each name will be used only once and must fit exactly into the number of boxes. One name has already been entered for you.

Flowers from the Prince

The prince has brought you flowers every day from Sunday until Saturday!

Every day he brought one of these:

On days starting with the letter T (like Tuesday) he also brought one of these:

Wednesday through Friday he also brought one of these:

On days with 6 letters (like Sunday) he also brought one of these:

Each flower lasts only three days and then must be discarded. For example, flowers received on Sunday must be discarded Wednesday. What does the bouquet of flowers look like on Saturday, after receiving and discarding?

A.

B.

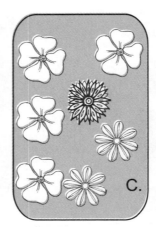

C.

D.

Out of This World

Have a friend or someone in your family help you create this story. Don't show them the story first! Ask them for the kind of word needed for each blank. Write the words in the blanks, then read the story out loud! Tip: Use a pencil so you can do it again with different words.

One day I was listening to _____ in front of my house.
(favorite song)

Suddenly, a large _____ stopped and a young man jumped out
(vehicle)

exclaiming, "My name is Prince _____ and you are listening to my
(boy's name)

favorite song!" The prince had _____ hair and was dressed in
(color)

_____ clothes. His _____ was shaped like a _____. Boy was he
(color)   (body part)   (fruit)

_____! He said that he was from _____. Suddenly, a monster
(adjective)   (planet)

_____ the size of a _____ appeared and threatened us with a
(snack food)   (something big)

_____! "Have no fear," the prince said bravely, "it is lunch time!"
(vegetable)

And he ate the monster in a single bite and drank _____ cups of
(large number)

_____. "Goodbye," he said as he got back into his vehicle, "I am
(beverage)

off to see _____ but I will return on _____."
(name of a friend)   (holiday)

Smarty Prince

A prince must be smart! The king has made this test for the prince. Can you figure out these phrases?

Example:

STAND
I

Answer: I understand,
because I is under STAND

po**FISH**nd

$\dfrac{long}{do}$

u
p
s
i
d
e
V

r
o
r o **a** d s
d
s

$\dfrac{rest}{your}$

LO head VE
heels

bad bad

you cont ol r

AALLLL

man
___
board

beating
beating beating
beating bush
beating
beating

hahandnd

wear
___
long

Jack

Kissing Frogs

You have to kiss a lot of frogs to find a prince! Can you find the frog on this page that will turn into a prince? It is the one that is in an oval and a triangle, but not in a rectangle.

Peculiar Prince Preferences

These girls use rules to pick a prince based on the letters in his name.
For each girl, you are given three examples that illustrate her rule.
Can you figure out which prince each girl likes from the choices?

Jennifer likes Prince Alex but not Prince Adam.
Jennifer likes Prince Max but not Prince Mark.
Jennifer likes Prince Rex but not Prince Andy.

Which Prince does Jennifer like?
A. Prince Randy   B. Prince Waldo   C. Prince Felix   D. Prince Peter

Audrey likes Prince Todd but not Prince Elroy
Audrey likes Prince Eli but not Prince Wesley
Audrey likes Prince Ian but not Prince Seth

Which Prince does Audrey like?
A. Prince Don   B. Prince Daniel   C. Prince Barry   D. Prince Ross

Grace likes Prince Isaac but not Prince Gary
Grace likes Prince Aaron but not Prince Lawrence
Grace likes Prince Coolidge but not Prince Bryan

Which Prince does Grace like?
A. Prince Ivan   B. Prince Lee   C. Prince George   D. Prince Robin

Heather likes Prince Tony but not Prince Robert
Heather likes Prince Timothy but not Prince Carlos
Heather likes Prince Tobias but not Prince Reuben

Which Prince does Heather like?
A. Prince Walter   B. Prince Keith   C. Prince Alfred   D. Prince Titus

A Very Handsome Prince

Copy each of the nine squares from the next page into this grid.
The letters and numbers tell you where each square belongs.

	A	B	C
1			
2			
3			

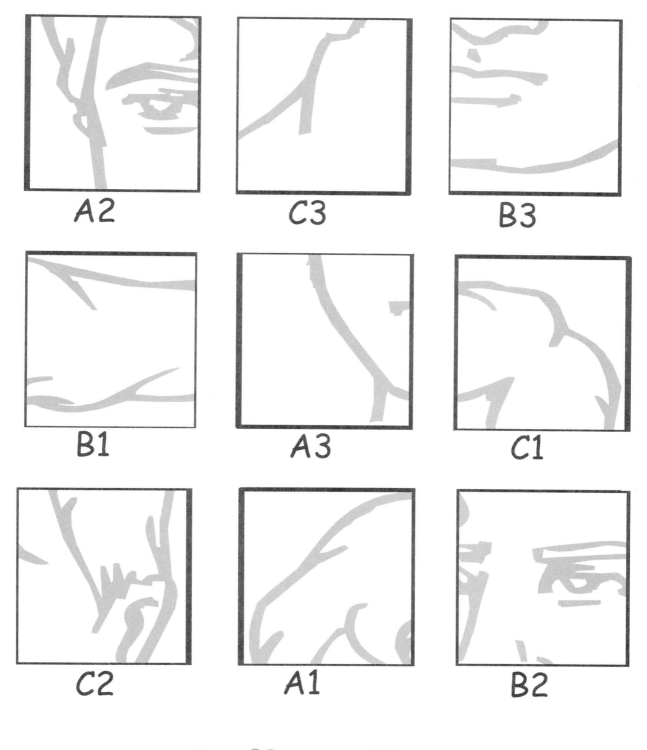

A2   C3   B3

B1   A3   C1

C2   A1   B2

Wedding Bells

It is time for the prince to marry the princess! Draw a line connecting the two halves of each wedding bell.

Chapter 7

Castles

Castles Around the World

Castles are found all over the world and were built to house and protect royal families. Find some of the countries where castles are located by looking up, down, across, backward, and diagonally. Some letters may be used more than once.

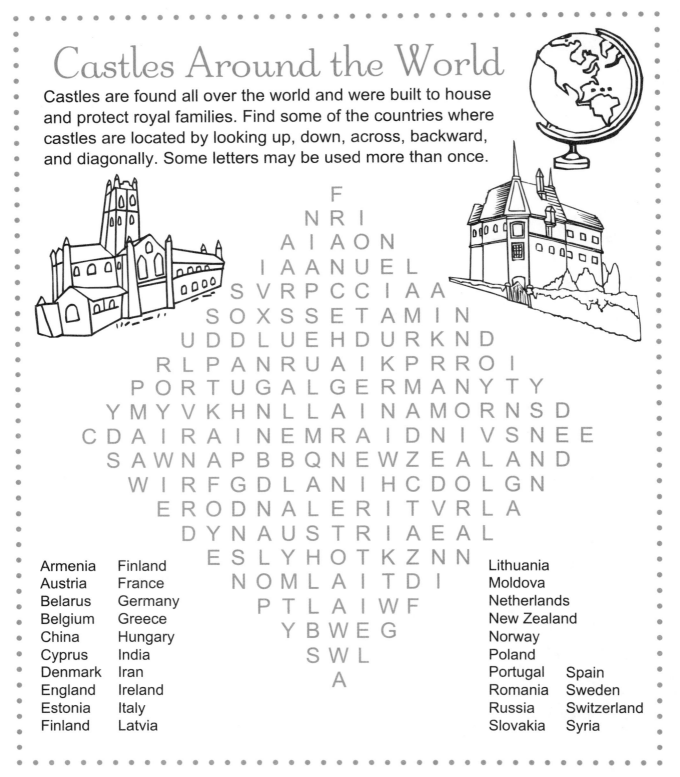

```
              F
          N R I
        A I A O N
      I A A N U E L
    S V R P C C I A A
    S O X S S E T A M I N
  U D D L U E H D U R K N D
  R L P A N R U A I K P R R O I
  P O R T U G A L G E R M A N Y T Y
  Y M Y V K H N L L A I N A M O R N S D
C D A I R A I N E M R A I D N I V S N E E
S A W N A P B B Q N E W Z E A L A N D
  W I R F G D L A N I H C D O L G N
  E R O D N A L E R I T V R L A
  D Y N A U S T R I A E A L
  E S L Y H O T K Z N N
  N O M L A I T D I
  P T L A I W F
  Y B W E G
  S W L
  A
```

Armenia	Finland	Lithuania	
Austria	France	Moldova	
Belarus	Germany	Netherlands	
Belgium	Greece	New Zealand	
China	Hungary	Norway	
Cyprus	India	Poland	
Denmark	Iran	Portugal	Spain
England	Ireland	Romania	Sweden
Estonia	Italy	Russia	Switzerland
Finland	Latvia	Slovakia	Syria

The Castle Flags

Cross out the one flag in each set that doesn't belong.

Royal Bricklayers

These bricklayers help build castles. Can you help them with these math problems?

Mason Jason needs to build a wall that is 3 bricks thick, 9 bricks high, and 100 bricks long. How many bricks does he need?

Can you help Mason Marvin put numbers on the blank bricks so that all the rows and columns add up to the same total?

3	4		4	2
	3		1	6
2		6		4
1		3	6	3
	4	1	3	5

Mason Mike needs to build a pyramid with eight bricks in the bottom layer. Each layer going up should have one less brick than the previous layer. The top layer should have only one brick. How many bricks does Mason Mike need?

Matching Bricks

This castle has thousands of bricks. Can you find where these four bricks match the samples below?

A. B. C. D.

Knockin' on the Castle Door

Unscramble the words to answer these knock-knock jokes.

Knock Knock!
Who's there?
Eiffel.
Eiffel who?

my
down
Eiffel
and
knee
hurt

Knock Knock!
Who's there?
Lettuce.
Lettuce who?

again
lettuce
tomorrow
try

Knock Knock!
Who's there?
Halibut.
Halibut who?

kiss
a
halibut

Knock Knock!
Who's there?
Jewel.
Jewel who?

know door Jewel open you if the

Knock Knock!
Who's there?
Ice cream soda.
Ice cream soda who?

whole world a soda are cream will Ice know what nut you

Knock Knock!
Who's there?
Dwayne.
Dwayne who?

bathtub the drowning I'm Dwayne

Knock Knock!
Who's there?
Island.
Island who?

your with roof my Island on parachute

Knock Knock!
Who's there?
Archibald.
Archibald who?

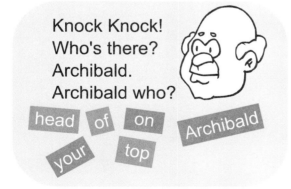

head of on Archibald your top

An aMAZEing Castle

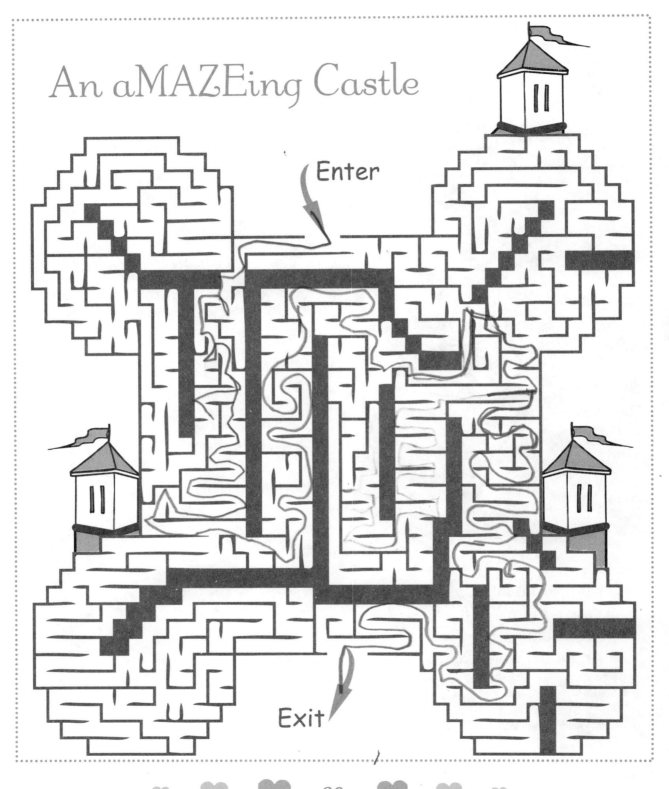

Enter

Exit

In the Kitchen

A Castle's kitchen needs to stock a lot of food to feed the royal family. These bags of grain need to be put into pots. Draw a line from each bag to a pot of the same size.

1 gallon = 4 quarts
1 quart = 2 pints
1 pint = 2 cups

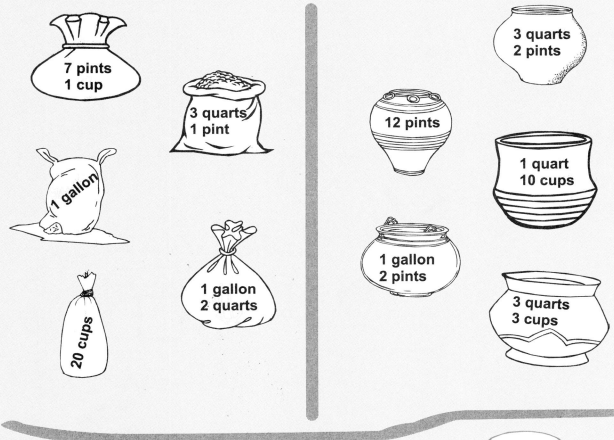

7 pints
1 cup

3 quarts
1 pint

1 gallon

20 cups

1 gallon
2 quarts

3 quarts
2 pints

12 pints

1 quart
10 cups

1 gallon
2 pints

3 quarts
3 cups

Farmer Adam gives Princess Pauline one gallon of apple juice every week. If she drinks one cup every morning and another cup every afternoon, how many cups will she have left at the end of the week?

Missing Pieces

Draw a line from each castle to its missing piece.

A Colorful Moat

Moats are usually filled with water and surround a castle for protection. This moat is filled with colors!

You can cross this moat by finding strings of letters that spell the names of colors. Start with a letter on the left side and then move right, up, or down. Some letters may be used more than once. One color crossing has been done for you. Can you find twelve more?

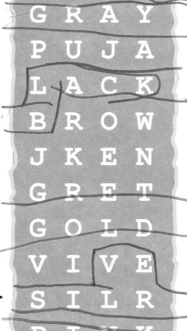

```
Y E A G
B L U E
O L O W
R A N F
M S G E
W H I T
K P L E
G R A Y
P U J A
L A C K
B R O W
J K E N
G R E T
G O L D
V I V E
S I L R
P I N K
```

Castle Furniture Store

What set of items can Princess Priscilla buy for exactly $92?

mirror $8

desk $64

What set of items can Princess Angela buy for exactly $162?

couch $128

chair $4

rug $2

lamp $1

bed $16

table $32

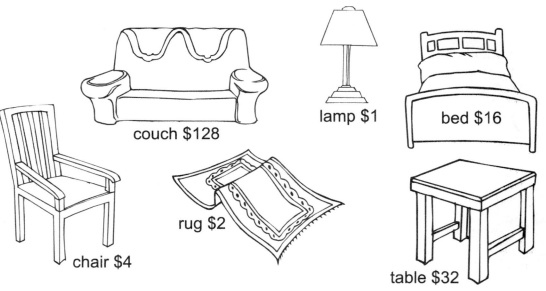

There is only one of each item available at this furniture store.

Chapter 8

Crowns and Tiaras

Tiara Maze

Start

Finish

One of a Kind

Can you find the one crown that does not exactly match any other crown on this page?

Is there an **even** or an **odd** number of crowns on this page? Do you have to count them to find out?

Comparing Tiaras

Princess Tiffany

Princess Lilly

Sophie's tiara has 3 more emeralds than Tiffany's. Veronica's tiara has twice as many emeralds as Lilly's, and half as many as Tiffany's. Whose tiara has the most emeralds?

Lilly's tiara has one more ruby than Tiffany's. Veronica's tiara has one more ruby than Sophie's. Tiffany's and Lilly's tiaras together have a total of 9 rubies. All four tiaras together have a total of 24 rubies. How many rubies are there in each tiara?

Princess Sophie

Princess Veronica

Tiffany's tiara has fewer diamonds than Veronica's. Lilly's tiara has more diamonds than Veronica's. Sophie's tiara has the least number of diamonds. Whose tiara has the most diamonds?

Whose Crown?

Can you figure out the names on these well-worn tags?

Princess Jaden

Princess Kristina

Princess Jessica

Princess Alexis

Princess Megan

Princess Samantha

Princess Michelle

Princess Erin

Princess Ashley

Portraits With a Crown

Complete these princess portraits:

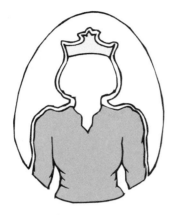

Happy Princess

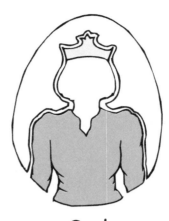

Sad Princess

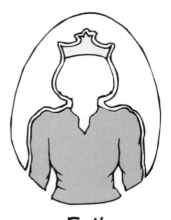

Evil Princess

Half and Half

Complete the other half of these crowns:

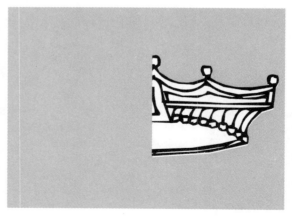

Jim the Gem Appraiser

Can you help Jim figure out the value
of the gems on each of these crowns?

Here is a guide to help you determine the values:

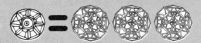

Diced Crowns

Drop two letters from CROWN and make a bovine:

_ _ _

Change one letter in CROWN and get a joker:

_ _ _ _ _

Change one letter in CROWN and turn a smile upside down:

_ _ _ _ _

Drop one letter from CROWN and it can fly:

_ _ _ _

Drop two letters from CROWN and propel a boat:

_ _ _ _

Tiara Jewels

This jeweler makes tiaras. Find the set of jewels below that exactly match these jewels needed for a tiara:

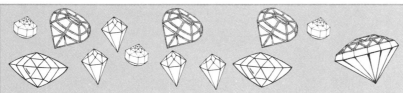

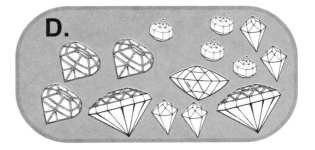

The Next Crown

Can you guess which crown comes after the first two?

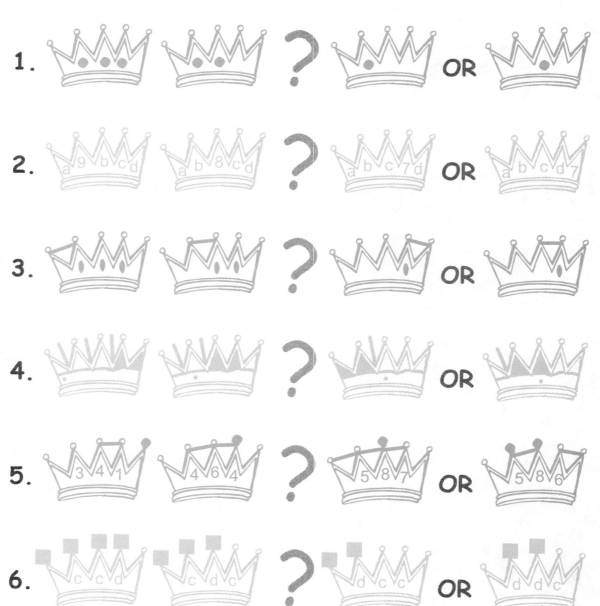

1.

2.

3.

4.

5.

6.

Chapter 9

Dresses and Dress Up

Dress Code

Circle the dress that
exactly matches
this one:

7 2
1 3 5 0 4
2
36 1 9 5 6 5
1
6 278532
8 1 2 8860
25 3 3 0 890 9

7 2
1 3 5 0 4
2
36 1 9 5 6 5
1
6 218532
8 1 2 8860
25 3 3 0 890 9

7 2
1 3 5 0 4
2
36 1 9 5 6 5
1
6 278532
8 2 8860
7
25 3 3 0 890 9

7 2
1 3 5 0 4
2
36 1 9 5 6 5
1
6 278532
8 1 2 8660
25 3 3 0 890 9

7 2
1 3 5 0 4
2
36 1 9 5 6 5
1
6 278532
8 1 2 8860
25 3 3 0 890 0

7 2
1 3 5 0 4
2
36 1 9 5 6 5
1
6 278532
8 1 5 8860
25 3 3 0 890 9

7 2
1 3 5 0 4
2
36 1 9 5 6 5
1
6 278532
8 1 2 8860
25 3 3 0 890 9

7 2
1 3 5 0 4
2
36 9 5 6 5
1
6 278532
8 1 2 8860
25 3 3 0 890 9

A Well-Worn Crossword Puzzle

Use the pictures as clues to this crossword puzzle.

Clothes Detective

Clothes can tell you a lot about a person. Can you fill in the blanks with a description of each person? Below is a list of letters to use. Each letter will be used only once, so cross 'em off after you use 'em.

AEPEMOAOFALERIOTBCLPRYCHESE RMALERLEURADLABALNELERINFNR

_ _ _ _ _ _ _ _ _ _ _ _ _ _

_ _ _ _ _

_ _ _ _ _ _ _

_ _ _ _ _ _ _ _ _ _ _

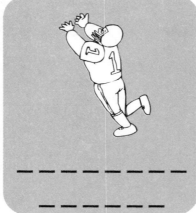

_ _ _ _ _ _ _ _ _
_ _ _ _ _ _

_ _ _ _ _ _

  98

Sew What?

These princesses like to sew their own dresses. Can you figure out which dress belongs to which princess? Untangle the thread from each princess to her dress. Write the correct name in each box.

Princess Madison

Princess Makayla

Princess Hannah

Princess Pauline

Dress Colors

Unscramble the colors on this page and see if you can find your favorite color.

EBEIG _ _ _ _ _

BURNGDUY _ _ _ _ _ _ _ _

RGYA _ _ _ _

WNORB _ _ _ _ _

RPEULP _ _ _ _ _ _

AYCN _ _ _ _

LRNVAEED _ _ _ _ _ _ _ _

PKIN _ _ _ _

ATN _ _ _

ILCLA _ _ _ _ _

LVSREI _ _ _ _ _ _

SAIUHCF _ _ _ _ _ _ _

AOMNOR _ _ _ _ _ _

UTQUSEIOR _ _ _ _ _ _ _ _ _

AKKHI _ _ _ _ _

YIOVR _ _ _ _ _

LEOIV _ _ _ _ _

ELOLWY _ _ _ _ _ _

BULE _ _ _ _

NEARGO _ _ _ _ _ _

NTMEAGA _ _ _ _ _ _ _

GLDO _ _ _ _

EDR _ _ _

IELOVT _ _ _ _ _ _

ITEHW _ _ _ _ _

ABKLC _ _ _ _ _

CHEPA _ _ _ _ _

GOIDIN _ _ _ _ _ _

LATE _ _ _ _

NGEER _ _ _ _ _

BONUS! Now unscramble the letters in the boxes to make a spotty pattern:

  100

Find all of the unscrambled colors and bonus words by looking up, down, across, backward and diagonally. Some letters may appear in more than one word.

```
    F Q T B N
  H C A E P P Y
  O Y T X S D P
  T A N E N O O
  U N E U L B O
X R J G K G O L D
S Q R A T I A I O
M U D M T V I V V
O B O I O E I S E F F
D T I N N T S H E O O
S M S D A I P C U I C
O A E I D H I U T G K
Y S R V G L W N F R T Q R
F D O M O N V K E A P H U
B R O W N L A E T G L L O
Y H N E G Q N R R R I U E
G W M Y U R V W O L L E Y
T G H I I K A H K C A L B
S J D H R O P Y I N C Y N
```

Dressed-Up Riddles

Answer the clues below and fill the letters into the grid. Work back and forth between the grid and the clues until you figure it out.

A. It is found between the hand and the arm

<u>w r i s t</u>
12 22 26 24 13

B. This can help if you have trouble walking.

<u>c a n e</u>
3 17 27 15

C. A vehicle that goes fast down a snow-covered hill.

<u>s l e d</u>
6 18 23 20

D. Small and round, they can make a necklace.

<u>B e a d s</u>
1 7 4 21 25

E. A meat commonly eaten at breakfast.

<u>S a u s a g e</u>
10 19 5 16 11 28 2

F. To strike.

<u>h i t</u>
14 8 9

Why did the tomato blush?

1D	2E	3B	4D	5E	6C	7D		8F	9F
B	e	c	a	u	s	e		i	t
10E	**11E**	**12A**		**13A**	**14F**	**15B**			
S	a	w		t					
16E	**17B**	**18C**	**19E**	**20C**					
21D	**22A**	**23C**	**24A**	**25D**	**26A**	**27B**	**28E**		

I'm a fancy dress,
and I start with G;
Wear me to the ball,
where the prince you will see.
What am I?

_ _ _ _ _

I make a bow on a dress,
if I'm tied in a knot;
I might be seen around a gift,
if they are brought.
What am I?

_ _ _ _

Embroidery

Can you trace the patterns on these dresses with one continuous line? Do not cross over or go back along any line.

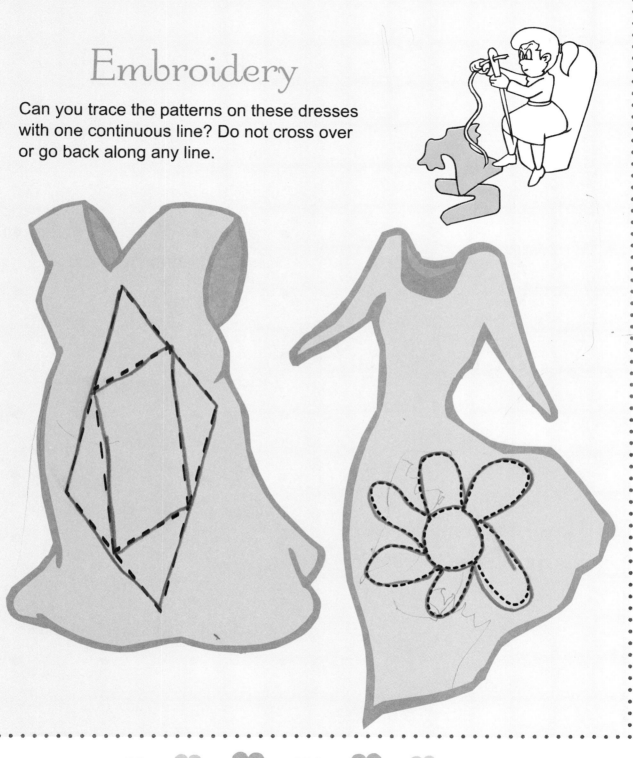

What to Wear?

Madeline has 5 pairs of shoes and 7 dresses. How many different combinations of shoes and dresses can Madeline wear? Assume that any of the shoes can be worn with any of the dresses.

Pretty Ugly

Divide the words into two groups by connecting the dots. One group should be "pretty" words and the other group "ugly" words. The puzzle has been started for you:

beautiful   attractive   yucky

lovely   repulsive   disgusting

fetching   charming   foul

cute   homely   beastly

elegant   hideous   frightful

appealing   pleasing   nasty

glamorous   alluring   handsome

Clueless Cloth

Dresses and clothes can be made with many different types of fabric. See if you can fit all of these fabrics into this clueless crossword puzzle. Each word is used only once, so cross it off the list when you've found the spot for it. One of the words is done for you.

3 Letters
FUR

4 Letters
FELT
JUTE
SILK
WOOL

5 Letters
DENIM
GAUZE
LINEN
NYLON
RAYON
SATIN
SUEDE
VINYL

6 Letters
BURLAP
CALICO
COTTON
VELVET

7 Letters
CHIFFON
FLANNEL
GINGHAM
LEATHER
SPANDEX
TAFFETA

8 Letters
CORDUROY

9 Letters
POLYESTER

10 Letters
SEERSUCKER
~~TERRYCLOTH~~

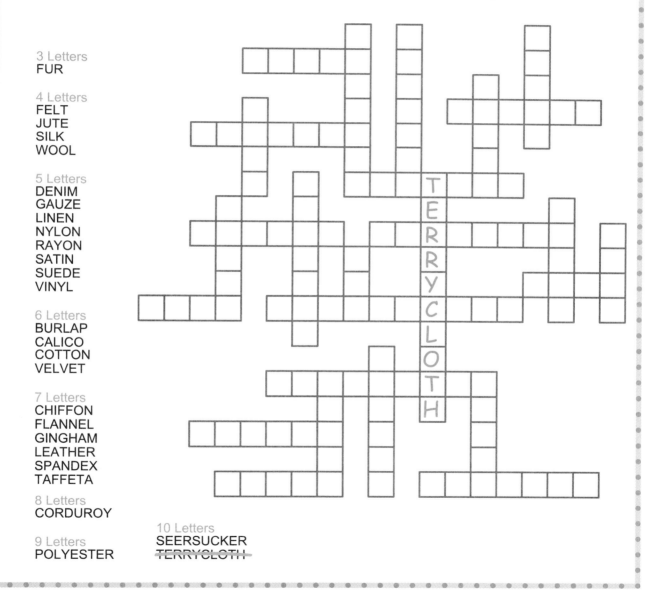

How Much for the Dress?

Can you find the correct price tag for this dress?
It will fit all of these rules:

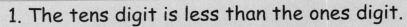

1. The tens digit is less than the ones digit.
2. The sum of both digits is less than 10.
3. It is an even number.
4. It does not have a 1.

$96

$87

$17

$33

$93

$26

$43

$32

$21

$28

$20

$95

$39

$63

$67

$14

$66

$47

$53

$98

$73

$79

$17

Which price is the lowest?
Which price is the highest?
Which price is exactly in the middle
(it has the same number of prices
above it as below it)?

Appendix A
Real-Life Princesses

Princesses really do exist! Here are some women who are princesses in real life.

Crown Princess Victoria of Sweden
Born July 14, 1977, she is the eldest child of King Carl XVI Gustaf and Queen Silvia. She is the heir apparent, thanks to a new law saying that the eldest child will inherit the throne regardless of sex. For the first time in history you no longer have to be male! Princess Victoria studied for two years at Yale University in the United States.

Crown Princess Mary of Denmark
Born February 5, 1972 in Australia, she is the wife of Crown Prince Frederik, the heir apparent to the Danish throne. She attended elementary school in Houston, Texas, where her father was a visiting professor. She met the prince in Australia at a party during the 2000 Summer Olympics.

Princess Letizia of Spain
Born September 15, 1972, she is the wife of Prince Felipe, the heir apparent to the Spanish throne. She was an award-winning TV anchorwoman and prime-time celebrity in Spain when she married Prince Felipe. She met the prince while reporting about an oil spill.

Masako, Crown Princess of Japan
Born December 9, 1963, she is the daughter of a senior diplomat. Masako traveled the world with her parents from early childhood. She graduated from a high school in Massachusetts where she achieved a perfect 4.0 grade point average. In 1985 she graduated at the top of her class from Harvard University. Masako refused the prince's marriage proposal twice before finally accepting!

Princess Esther Kamatari of Burundi
Born in 1951, she is a writer, model, and exiled princess. She grew up in Burundi, but her father (the king) was overthrown in 1964. The princess fled the country and settled in Paris where she became involved in humanitarian work to help the people of Burundi.

Diana, Princess of Wales

Born July 1, 1961, she was the first wife of Charles, Prince of Wales, and perhaps the most famous woman in the world. Lady Diana was working as an assistant at a kindergarten in England before she married the prince. The two divorced in 1996. Diana was well known for her support of charity projects, including campaigns against the use of landmines and helping the victims of AIDS. She died in a tragic car accident in 1997.

Princess Grace of Monaco

Born November 12, 1929, she became a princess when she married Prince Rainier III of Monaco in 1956. Before marrying the prince, Grace Kelly was an Academy Award–winning American film actress. She never acted after becoming a princess and had three children. Princess Grace died after being in a car accident in 1982.

Appendix B
Fun Web Sites

www.funbrain.com
Loaded with brainy (but really fun) games for kids of all ages.

www.funster.com
Compete against friends at this web site with multiplayer word games and other puzzles. Created by the author of this book!

disney.go.com/princess
Play games with all of your favorite princesses, including Snow White and Cinderella.

www.bonus.com
Chock full of fun games of all types. Check out the Family section that includes Arts and Crafts.

www.angelinaballerina.com
Dress up Angelina, the ballerina mouse, and help her stage a beautiful ballet.

www.funschool.com
The emphasis is definitely on fun at this web site with a variety of games for every grade.

www.barbie.com
Dress up your favorite dolls and decorate their rooms. Hint: many spots on the screen can be clicked for more fun.

www.bbc.co.uk/schools/famouspeople/standard/pocahontas
The true story of Pocahontas, native American Indian princess.

www.i-dressup.com
For those in love with fashion, style, and dress-up games!

www.birthdaypartyideas.com/html/princess.html
Ideas for how to throw a princess birthday party.

Find the Pictures

6

3

4

5

2

7

9

1

8

Chapter 1

page 2 •
Mixed-up Kitchen

1. kettle
2. knife
3. oven
4. stove
5. spoon
6. fork
7. bowl
8. plate
9. pitcher
10. pot
11. cup
12. pan
13. table

page 4 •
The Magic Wand

Drop the first letter from...
...and turn it into drops from the sky.
TRAIN & RAIN

Drop the last two letters from...
...and turn it into the event where Cinderella and the Prince meet.
BALLET & BALL

Drop the first two letters from...

...and turn it into gorillas.
GRAPES & APES

Drop the first letter from this...
...and turn it into something heartfelt.
GLOVE & LOVE

Drop the first letter from these...

and turn it into something cold
DICE & ICE

Drop the first letter from a...

...and turn it into a garden tool.
SHOE & HOE

Drop the last letter from...
...and turn it into a drink made with leaves.
TEAR & TEA

Drop the last letter from this...

...and turn it into a baby bear.
CUBE & CUB

Drop the first letter from...
...and turn it into what you breathe.
HAIR & AIR

Drop the first two letters from a...
...and turn it into a creative work.
HEART & ART

Drop the first letter from these...
...and turn them into noisemakers
THORNS & HORNS

Puzzle Answers

page 6 • Riding to the Ball

page 7 • Dancing by the Numbers

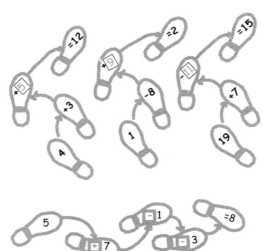

page 8 • The Last Dance

Cinderella must leave after Momma Mambo.

page 9 • The Confused Prince

The center dots are the same size. In both cases, the vertical lines are the same size. Don't believe it? Then measure them with a ruler!

page 10 • If the Shoe Fits, Wear It!

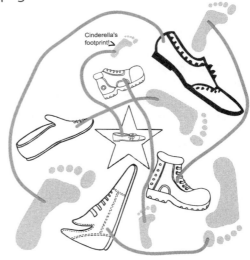

page 11 • **Wedding Seating**

The Marquis
of Macadamia

The Countess
of Calypso

The Earl
of Eaton

The Duchess
of Duncan

page 12 • **Wedding Cake**

page 12 • **Cryptic Conclusion**

AND THEY LIVED HAPPILY
EVER AFTER...

Chapter 2

page 14 • **My Real Name**

M A T O A K A
1 2 3 4 5 6 7

page 14 • **Where I'm From**

EMVSIMSE
REMSGIMS
MENSMIAE

VIRGINIA

page 16 • **The Path to Jamestown**

page 15 • **The Time Machine**

The year is 1700, what has not yet been invented:
- [ ] pencil
- [x] lightning rod
- [ ] toilet

The year is 1800, what has not yet been invented:
- [x] lawn mower
- [ ] steam engine
- [ ] piano

The year is 1850, what has not yet been invented:
- [ ] batteries
- [x] zipper
- [ ] Morse code

The year is 1900, what has not yet been invented:
- [ ] telephone
- [ ] light bulb
- [x] antibiotics

The year is 1950, what has not yet been invented:
- [x] Internet
- [ ] television
- [ ] computer

The year is 1990, what has not yet been invented:
- [ ] cell phone
- [ ] pocket calculator
- [x] DVD movies

page 17 • **Fair Trades**

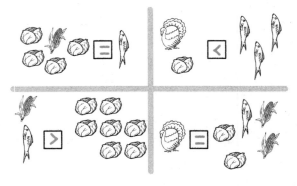

    114

Puzzle Answers

page 18 • **John Smith and Pocahontas**

A. A large stream of water.
R I V E R
17 22 63 27 6

B. A group of players on the same side.
T E A M
4 24 39 13

C. Title at the top of a newspaper.
H E A D L I N E
11 60 48 43 28 29 42 31

D. What you get when you boil water.
S T E A M
54 21 36 41 23

E. Ten cents.
D I M E
40 51 15 53

F. 12 inches.
F O O T
20 56 16 25

G. Opposite of low.
H I G H
26 62 66 47

H. Bird's home.
N E S T
52 12 55 34

I. Do it at a red light.
S T O P
9 10 32 49

J. To turn over.
F L I P
30 61 64 50

K. Stay out of sight.
H I D E
59 8 37 46

L. Not no.
Y E S
18 38 3

M. Between fourth and sixth.
F I F T H
33 2 57 44 45

N. Capable of burning.
H O T
35 19 58

O. Bees make it.
H O N E Y
1 5 65 14 7

1O	2M	3L	4B	5O	6A	7O		8K	9I		
H	I	S	T	O	R	Y		I	S		
10I	11C	12H		13B	14O	15E	16F	17A	18L		
T	H	E		M	E	M	O	R	Y		
19N	20F		21D	22A	23D	24B		25F	26G	27A	
O	F		T	I	M	E,		T	H	E	
28C	29C	30J	31C		32I	33M		34H	35N	36D	
L	I	F	E		O	F		T	H	E	
37K	38L	39B	40E		41D	42C	43C		44M	45M	46K
D	E	A	D,		A	N	D		T	H	E
47G	48C	49I	50J	51E	52H	53E	54D	55H		56F	57M
H	A	P	P	I	N	E	S	S		O	F
58N	59K	60C		61J	62G	63A	64J	65O	66G		
T	H	E		L	I	V	I	N	G	.	

Pocahontas was 12 years old when she rescued John Smith.

page 20 • **Missing Flowers**

A.   B.   C.

D.   E.   F.

   115

page 21 • **A Vase for Pocahontas**

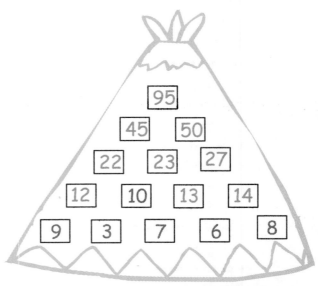

page 22 • **Mathematical Teepee**

page 23 • **A Corny Pyramid**

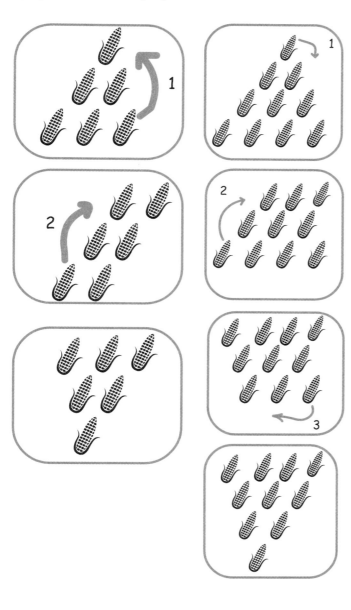

page 24 • **Sailing to England**

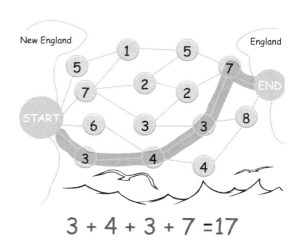

3 + 4 + 3 + 7 = 17

Chapter 3

page 26 • Interesting Combinations

blast**off**	down**town**
offspring	break**down**
cut**off**	melt**down**
foot**ball**	red **cross**
foot**print**	**cross**word
bare**foot**	**cross**walk
bottle cap	sun**burn**
hub**cap**	sun**flower**
ice**cap**	sun**set**

---

kick**stand**	camp**ground**
sidekick	**under**ground
kick**ball**	ground **floor**
bus **stop**	saw**dust**
stopwatch	**dust**pan
doorstop	dust **storm**
rail**road**	green**house**
roadrunner	winter**green**
roadblock	ever**green**
light**house**	outer **space**
light**weight**	**parking** space
flashlight	space **shuttle**

page 28 • Mathmagic Mermaid

The net result of all the steps is to multiply your number by 10 and add 7. Thus, your number will be in the tens digit and a 7 will be in the ones digit.

page 29 • Transform

There are many possible solutions. Here are our answers:

BIRD to BEAR

B I R D
B I N D
B E N D
B E A D
B E A R

CAT to DOG

C A T
C O T
D O T
D O G

COW to PIG

C O W
B O W
B O G
B I G
P I G

MOON to MARS

M O O N
M O R N
M O R E
M A R E
M A R S

HAND to FOOT

H A N D
B A N D
B O N D
F O N D
F O O D
F O O T

page 30 • Fishy Friends

SHARK
DARTER
GUPPY
BLUEGILL
FLUKE
CRAPPIE
CHUB
GOBY
COD

FLOUNDER
YELLOWTAIL
GOLDFISH
CATFISH
MINNOW
ALBACORE
SOLE
TUNA
CARP
HALIBUT
WALLEYE
HADDOCK
ANCHOVY
SALMON
GUITARFISH
ANGEL

PIKE
MARLIN
GRUNION
GROUPER
HERRING
BASS
PERCH
STURGEON
BARRACUDA
BULLHEAD
TROUT
MACKEREL
SNAPPER
SARDINE
MUSKIE
PARROTFISH

page 32 • Save the Prince

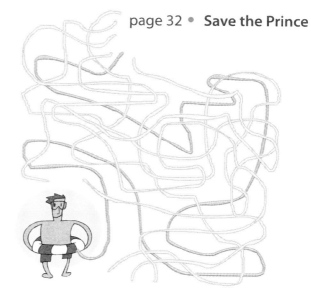

   119

page 33 • Predictions

page 35 • Where is My Prince?

page 34 • Mermaid Riddles

What fish is the most valuable?
A goldfish.

Why are fish so smart?
Because they live in schools.

What fish likes bubble gum?
A blowfish.

What fish is the most famous?
A starfish.

Why is it so easy to weigh a fish?
They have their own scales.

page 36 • Treasure Watcher

page 38 • **Good Fairies**

page 39 • **Fairy Gifts**

page 40 • **What's in a Name?**

Here are some of the words found in SLEEPING BEAUTY:

able ail angel ate base bee belt big blue bus eagle else eye gas get glue guy lab lean lip nail net paint past peanut pet pine plan plus put sang set slant snug spit staple stay suit tail tea tiny tip ugly up yes

There are many more possible words. How many did you find?

page 41 • **Spinning Wheel Spell**

PRINCESS   BEWARE!

SPINNING   WHEELS   POISONOUS!
                ARE

page 42 • **Dreaming Beauty**

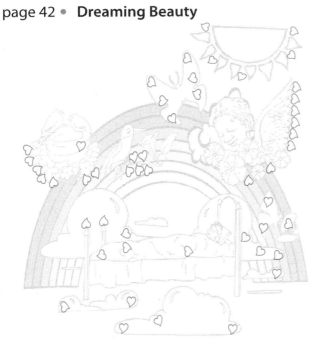

page 43 • **One Hundred Years**

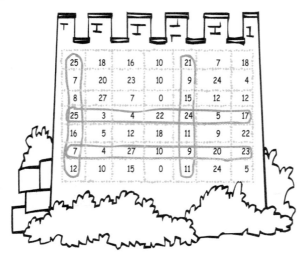

page 44 • **Double E**

Puzzle Answers

page 46 • **The Path to Sleeping Beauty**

page 48 • **A Message from the Prince**

	1	2	3	4	5	6	7
♥	I		H	A	V	E	
♣	F	O	U	N	D		
♦	M	Y		T	R	U	E
♠	L	O	V	E			

page 47 • **Castle Maze**

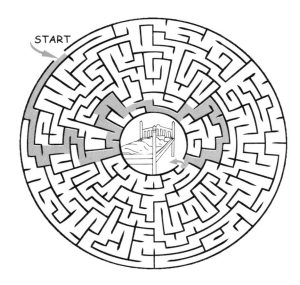

Chapter 5

page 50 • **Mirror, Mirror**

SNOW   WHITE
IS   A
THOUSAND
TIMES   FAIRER
THAN   YOU!

page 52 • **The Secret Answer**

   **124**

page 53 • **Twisty Walk**

page 54 • **Things in the Forest**

page 55 • **Seven of Everything**

There are only 6 of these:

There are 8 of these:

page 56 • **Snow White's Crossword**

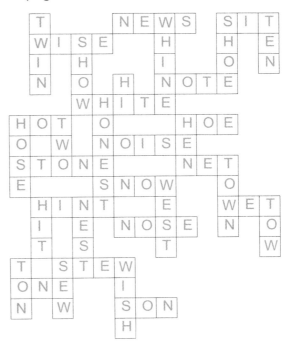

Puzzle Answers

page 58 • **Doesn't Belong**

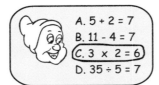

A. 5 + 2 = 7
B. 11 - 4 = 7
C. 3 × 2 = 6
D. 35 ÷ 5 = 7

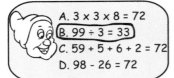

A. 3 × 3 × 8 = 72
B. 99 ÷ 3 = 33
C. 59 + 5 + 6 + 2 = 72
D. 98 - 26 = 72

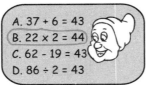

A. 37 + 6 = 43
B. 22 × 2 = 44
C. 62 - 19 = 43
D. 86 ÷ 2 = 43

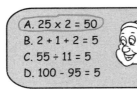

A. 25 × 2 = 50
B. 2 + 1 + 2 = 5
C. 55 ÷ 11 = 5
D. 100 - 95 = 5

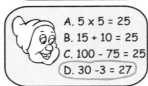

A. 5 × 5 = 25
B. 15 + 10 = 25
C. 100 - 75 = 25
D. 30 -3 = 27

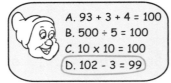

A. 93 + 3 + 4 = 100
B. 500 ÷ 5 = 100
C. 10 × 10 = 100
D. 102 - 3 = 99

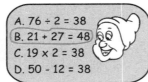

A. 76 ÷ 2 = 38
B. 21 + 27 = 48
C. 19 × 2 = 38
D. 50 - 12 = 38

page 59 • **The Poisoned Apple**

page 60 • **Wedding Cake**

Table A:
1. Diane
2. Therese
3. Steve
4. Donnie
5. Suzanne

Table B:
1. Mary
2. Dave
3. Violet

Table C:
1. Emma
2. Shawn
3. Nick
4. Laura

Chapter 6

page 62 • Prince Names from A to Z

Evan	Timothy
Samuel	Marcus
Logan	Noah
Paul	Ulysses
Quincy	Ian
Hunter	Franklin
Kenneth	Raymond
Carlos	Jason
Dylan	Andrew
Oscar	William
Garrett	Xavier
Yannick	Victor
Zachary	Benjamin

page 64 • Flowers from the Prince

D.

page 63 • Clueless Princes

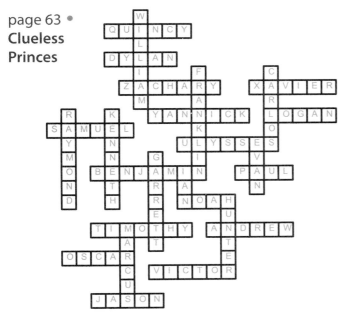

page 65 • Out of This World

Everybody will have a different story. Here's ours:

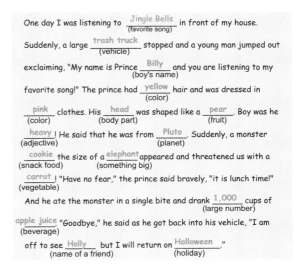

One day I was listening to _Jingle Bells_ in front of my house.
(favorite song)

Suddenly, a large _trash truck_ stopped and a young man jumped out
(vehicle)

exclaiming, "My name is Prince _Billy_ and you are listening to my
(boy's name)

favorite song!" The prince had _yellow_ hair and was dressed in
(color)

pink clothes. His _head_ was shaped like a _pear_. Boy was he
(color)   (body part)   (fruit)

heavy ! He said that he was from _Pluto_ . Suddenly, a monster
(adjective)   (planet)

cookie the size of a _elephant_ appeared and threatened us with a
(snack food)   (something big)

carrot ! "Have no fear," the prince said bravely, "it is lunch time!"
(vegetable)

And he ate the monster in a single bite and drank _1,000_ cups of
(large number)

apple juice "Goodbye," he said as he got back into his vehicle, "I am
(beverage)

off to see _Holly_ but I will return on _Halloween_ ."
(name of a friend)   (holiday)

page 66 • **Smarty Prince**

a big fish in a little pond

crossroads

long overdue

upside down

you're under arrest

head over heels in love

too bad

you are out of control

all in all

man overboard

beating around the bush

hand in hand

jack-in-the-box

long underwear

page 68 • **Kissing Frogs**

page 69 • **Peculiar Prince Preferences**

Jennifer likes C. Prince Felix because his name ends with the letter X.

Audrey likes A. Prince Don because his name has three letters.

Grace likes B. Prince Lee because his name has a double letter.

Heather likes D. Prince Titus because his name starts with the letter T.

page 70 • **A Very Handsome Prince**

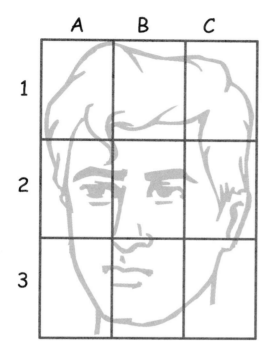

page 72 • **Wedding Bells**

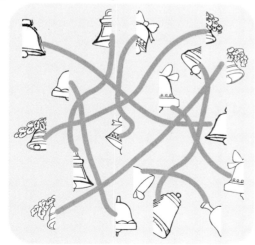

129

Chapter 7

page 74 • Castles Around the World

page 75 • The Castle Flags

Each flag must have 2 circles and 1 triangle.

Each flag must have all of these letters: PRINCESS

Each flag must have numbers that add up to ten.

Each flag must have an animal

Each flag must have seven dots.

page 76 • Royal Bricklayers

Mason Jason needs 2,700 bricks.
(9 X 3 X 100)

Here are the numbers Mason Marvin needs to put on the bricks:

3	4	7	4	2
7	3	3	1	6
2	2	6	6	4
1	7	3	6	3
7	4	1	3	5

Mason Mike needs 36 bricks.
(8+7+6+5+4+3+2+1)

page 77 • Matching Bricks

page 78 • Knockin' on the Castle Door

Knock Knock!
Who's there?
Lettuce.
Lettuce who?
Lettuce try again tomorrow!

Knock Knock!
Who's there?
Eiffel.
Eiffel who?
Eiffel down and hurt my knee!

Knock Knock!
Who's there?
Halibut.
Halibut who?
Halibut a kiss!

Knock Knock!
Who's there?
Jewel.
Jewel who?
Jewel know if you open the door!

Knock Knock!
Who's there?
Ice cream soda.
Ice cream soda who?
Ice cream soda whole world will know what a nut you are!

Knock Knock!
Who's there?
Dwayne.
Dwayne who?
Dwayne the bathtub I'm drowning!

Knock Knock!
Who's there?
Island.
Island who?
Island on your roof with my parachute!

Knock Knock!
Who's there?
Archibald.
Archibald who?
Archibald on top of your head?

page 80 • An aMAZEing Castle

page 81 • In the Kitchen

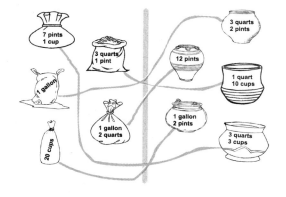

Princess Pauline will have two cups of apple juice left at the end of the week.

page 82 • **Missing Pieces**

page 84 • **Castle Furniture Store**

Princess Priscilla will buy the desk, bed, chair, and mirror.

Princess Angela will buy the couch, table, and rug.

page 83 •
A Colorful Moat

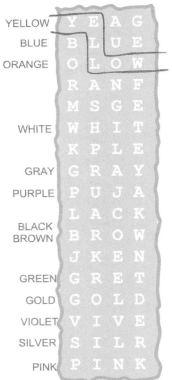

YELLOW
BLUE
ORANGE

WHITE

GRAY
PURPLE

BLACK
BROWN

GREEN
GOLD
VIOLET
SILVER
PINK

Chapter 8

Start

page 86 • **Tiara Maze**

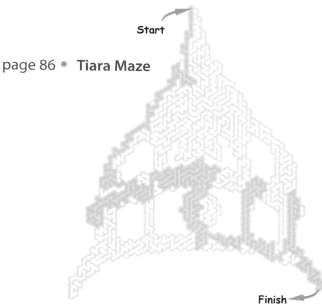

Finish

page 87 • **One of a Kind**

There must be an odd number of crowns because they are all in pairs (an even number) except for one (making the total an odd number).

page 88 • **Comparing Tiaras**

Princess Sophie's tiara has the most emeralds.

Princess Tiffany's tiara has 4 rubies.
Princess Lilly's tiara has 5 rubies.
Princess Veronica's tiara has 8 rubies.
Princess Sophie's tiara has 7 rubies.

Princess Lilly's tiara has the most diamonds.

page 89 • **Whose Crown?**

Puzzle Answers

page 90 • **Portraits with a Crown**

Happy Princess   Sad Princess   Evil Princess

page 90 • **Half and Half**

page 91 • **Jim the Gem Appraiser**

First, determine the value of each gem:

 = $120   = $20

 = $40   = $180

Then you can determine the values of the gems in each crown:

$120

$840

$280

$460

page 92 • **Diced Crowns**

 Drop two letters from CROWN and make a bovine: COW

 Change one letter in CROWN and get a joker: CLOWN

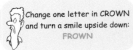 Change one letter in CROWN and turn a smile upside down: FROWN

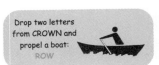 Drop two letters from CROWN and propel a boat: ROW

 Drop one letter from CROWN and it can fly: CROW

page 93 • **Tiara Jewels**

page 94 • **The Next Crown**

Chapter 9

page 96 •
Dress Code

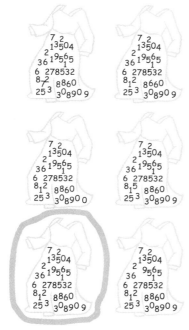

page 98 • **Clothes Detective**

CHEERLEADER   NURSE   BALLERINA

POLICEMAN   FOOTBALL PLAYER   FARMER

page 99 • **Sew What?**

page 97 • **A Well-Worn Crossword Puzzle**

page 100 • Dress Colors

BEIGE	IVORY
BURGUNDY	OLIVE
GRAY	YELLOW
BROWN	BLUE
PURPLE	ORANGE
CYAN	MAGENTA
LAVENDER	GOLD
PINK	RED
TAN	VIOLET
LILAC	WHITE
SILVER	BLACK
FUCHSIA	PEACH
MAROON	INDIGO
TURQUOISE	TEAL
KHAKI	GREEN

POLKA DOTS

page 102 • Dressed-Up Riddles

A. It is found between the hand and the arm

W R I S T
12 22 26 24 13

B. This can help if you have trouble walking.

C A N E
3 17 27 15

C. A vehicle that goes fast down a snow-covered hill.

S L E D
6 18 23 20

D. Small and round, they can make a necklace.

B E A D S
1 7 4 21 25

E. A meat commonly eaten at breakfast.

S A U S A G E
10 19 5 16 11 28 2

F. To strike.

H I T
14 8 9

1D B	2E E	3B C	4D A	5E U	6C S	7D E		8F I	9F T
10E S	11E A	12A W		13A T	14F H	15B E			
16E S	17B A	18C L	19E A	20C D					
21D D	22A R	23C E	24A S	25D S	26A I	27B N	28E G	.	

GOWN, RIBBON

page 103 • Embroidery

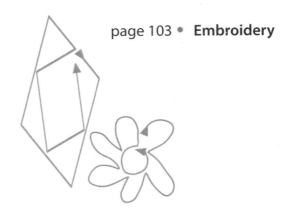

page 104 • What to Wear?

Each dress can be worn with 5 possible pairs of shoes. There are 7 dresses. So the answer is 7 X 5, or 35 different combinations.

page 104 • Pretty Ugly

page 104 • Clueless Cloth

page 106 • How Much for the Dress?

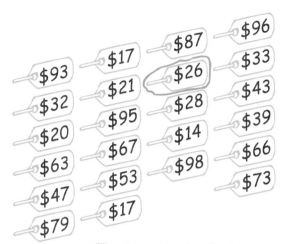

The lowest price is $14
The highest price is $98
The middle price is $47

The Everything® Kids' Series

The Everything® Kids' Animal Puzzle & Activity Book
1-59337-305-8

The Everything® Kids' Baseball Book, 4th Ed.
1-59337-614-6

The Everything® Kids' Bible Trivia Book
1-59337-031-8

The Everything® Kids' Bugs Book
1-58062-892-3

The Everything® Kids' Cars and Trucks
Puzzle and Activity Book
1-59337-703-7

The Everything® Kids' Christmas Puzzle & Activity Book
1-58062-965-2

The Everything® Kids' Cookbook
1-58062-658-0

The Everything® Kids' Crazy Puzzles Book
1-59337-361-9

The Everything® Kids' Dinosaurs Book
1-59337-360-0

The Everything® Kids' First Spanish
Puzzle and Activity Book
1-59337-717-7

The Everything® Kids' Gross Hidden Pictures Book
1-59337-615-4

The Everything® Kids' Gross Jokes Book
1-59337-448-8

The Everything® Kids' Gross Mazes Book
1-59337-616-2

The Everything® Kids' Gross Puzzle & Activity Book
1-59337-447-X

The Everything® Kids' Halloween Puzzle &
Activity Book
1-58062-959-8

The Everything® Kids' Hidden Pictures Book
1-59337-128-4

The Everything® Kids' Horses Book
1-59337-608-1

The Everything® Kids' Joke Book
1-58062-686-6

The Everything® Kids' Knock Knock Book
1-59337-127-6

The Everything® Kids' Learning Spanish Book
1-59337-716-9

The Everything® Kids' Math Puzzles Book
1-58062-773-0

The Everything® Kids' Mazes Book
1-58062-558-4

The Everything® Kids' Money Book
1-58062-685-8

The Everything® Kids' Nature Book
1-58062-684-X

The Everything® Kids' Pirates Puzzle and Activity Book
1-59337-607-3

The Everything® Kids' Princess Puzzle and Activity Book
1-59337-704-5

The Everything® Kids' Puzzle Book
1-58062-687-4

The Everything® Kids' Riddles & Brain Teasers Book
1-59337-036-9

The Everything® Kids' Science Experiments Book
1-58062-557-6

The Everything® Kids' Sharks Book
1-59337-304-X

The Everything® Kids' Soccer Book
1-58062-642-4

The Everything® Kids' Travel Activity Book
1-58062-641-6

All titles are $6.95 or $7.95 unless otherwise noted.

Available wherever books are sold!
To order, call 800-258-0929, or visit us at www.adamsmedia.com
Everything® and everything.com® are registered trademarks of F+W Publications, Inc.
Prices subject to change without notice.